Cosy Autumn

A SEASONAL GUIDE

Melanie Steele

Copyright © 2023 by Melanie Steele.

All rights reserved. No part of this book may be used or reproduced in any form whatsoever without written permission except in the case of brief quotations in critical articles or reviews.

Printed in the United Kingdom.

Follow me on Instagram @melaniesteeleauthor

MELANIESTEELE

Book design by Melanie Steele
Cover design by Melanie Steele

First Edition : August 2023

INTRODUCTION

I was born in September, so I'm a bit biased when it comes to Autumn.

Autumn for me means many things. When I was younger, it always meant the start of a new school year and scouring the shops for new stationary (I still love that to be honest) and thus it always felt like a beginning time- not three quarters of the way through the year time! It seemed to be a time for new possibilities, new ideas and best of all- a time for being home.

As a huge introvert there's nothing better to me than being at home cosied up reading a book, watching a film or baking something. That is my happy place.

Now I'm all grown up (Sort of) with a home of my own I can really go to town- think pumpkin decorations, candles, blankets over the sofa and smells of baking wafting through the downstairs. It brings me so much joy, and if you're reading this I imagine you feel the same.

I know I'm not alone in my love of Autumn, and with the meteoric rise of Halloween here in the UK (Fuelled largely by our American friends on social media showing us their TJ Maxx, Michaels and Target hauls) Its evident that more and more of us are celebrating this time of year, and of course Halloween!

I felt drawn to write about this wonderful season- not a huge great novel, but a fun guide with ideas, recipes and inspiration for my fellow cosy lovers out there to refer to when they need a dose of Autumn magic.

I hope you enjoy this little guide- If you do I'd love for you to follow me on Instagram @melaniesteeleauthor

CHAPTER 1

Morning Routine

Ah, the morning routine. Anyone who, like me, grew up in the era of Youtube beauty gurus is more than familiar with morning routines. I was obsessed with those videos! Everything was so glossy, so perfect. The pyjamas were cute, the kitchens where they made their hot chocolate were huge, and they always had time to journal their thoughts whilst baking something delicious. They were just so... dreamy, aspirational and polished.

Now I'm older, I think about just how awkward those morning routine videos must have been to film. Imagine having to get up, get picture perfect ready, put on your best pyjamas... then go back to bed, pull the covers up and cue someone to start filming as you "wake up" and go get a coffee. It's bonkers!

However, part of me still yearns for a morning routine like that. Especially in the Autumn. The cool mornings where its still a bit dark (If you're a morning person like me who doesn't sleep past 6am, ever) and you're already pondering whether its going to be a crisp cool sort of day, or a wet and windy one. Here in the UK, the odds are always 50/50.

If you search "Morning Routine" on Pinterest, you will be inundated with pretty pins luring you to click them with promises of said routines being "Easy", "Perfect" and "Dreamy" The pins always seem to have pictures of fluffy socks and mugs of coffee that my brain is incapable of resisting.

The trouble is that when I read the blog post within, I start to feel overwhelmed... and maybe a bit *jealous*. The sheer amount of activities these bloggers seem to get done before their day starts is astounding! For context I am married and child free. I theoretically have more than enough time in the morning, undisturbed, to do *all the things* BUT I just don't do them. I know I'm not the only one guilty of this either.

The reason I don't is very simple- whilst my dreamy side of me loves the idea of a polished morning routine, and berates me for not having it, deep down I just *don't want* to have a 10 step routine. So if that's what you were hoping for here, then sorry. Go log onto Pinterest instead!

So that begs the question, what *do* I want my morning routine to look like?

For me, a person with more ideas than time, I like to keep it flexible. I have a selection of things I could do, and I let myself choose from the morning routine menu if you will, each day. That way I'm not overwhelmed, or stressing that I didn't do a particular thing that morning.

My Autumn Morning Routine- The Non Negotiable

I always start my morning with Coffee. (Sorry Tea lovers)

Popping a seasonally appropriate coffee pod in my coffee machine is a nice little touch for this time of year, and makes a change from my regular coffee pod of choice. Most brands come out with at least one seasonal flavour, including supermarket own brands. There's less choice for my filter coffee fans, but if instant coffee is your thing there's a huge selection of flavoured coffees.

Now I know coffee syrups are super popular for adding to coffee, but they can be expensive and full of sugar or sweetener. Don't get me wrong, I love a Starbucks PSL more than anyone I know (More on that later) but I certainly wouldn't drink one every day- for both health and financial reasons.

Instead, I like to make a flavoured creamer- its not actually made with cream but its what the Americans call it so lets go with it! You can use any milk you like- dairy or plant based, and it has much less sugar, and no artificial sweeteners.

Pumpkin Spice Coffee Creamer Recipe

- 200ml Milk of Choice
- 2 Tbsp Maple Syrup
- 1.5 Tsp Pumpkin Pie Spice (See note below to make your own)
- 1.5 Tsp Vanilla Extract
- Pumpkin Pie Spice Blend
- 1 Tsp Cinammon
- ¼ Tsp Nutmeg (Ground)
- ¼ Tsp Ginger
- 1/8 Tsp Cloves

1. Put the milk in a saucepan and warm gently- you don't want to boil it.
2. Add in the rest of the ingredients and whisk till combined.
3. Allow to cool, then store in an airtight container such as a jar or sterile bottle.
4. Will generally keep for 1 week in the fridge, but do check before using.

You can add 1-2Tbsp of pumpkin puree to this recipe, but as its an expensive ingredient here in the UK (due to it being imported), there's no need to open a tin just for 2 tablespoons. Unless you happen to be baking with it that day!

CHAPTER 2

Autumn Activities

If you put "Autumn (or Fall) activities" into a Pinterest search, you will be met with an abundance of cute infographics full of suggestions. However, I find these suggestions are obviously geared towards our American friends with things like "Visit a Pumpkin Patch" (Not really a common thing here in the UK) or "Make Apple Cider" (Again, non alcoholic apple cider not a thing here) They are also very family (read:children) orientated- making us child-free folks feel a bit lost. No one wants to be the adult couple without kids at a family day out.

So instead, I have curated a list of more adult centric, and British, Autumn activities. I hope these will inspire you to come up with your own, no matter who you are, or where you live!

Day Trip
My Husband and I are both National Trust members, and we like to go on day trips to sites near us. This time of year, Stonehenge and Avebury are top of my list. What can I say, I love a good stone circle and all the history that goes with them! If you're not quite as obssessed with stone circles as I am, here are a few more suggestions!

A Local Castle

Castles are amazing year round, but there's something extra special (possibly spooky) about visiting one in Autumn/Winter time. I find myself imagining its former occupants gathering around a fireplace, engaging in traditional hobbies and games. The kitchen busy with staff making an Autumn feast, and warming the beds whilst also trying to avoid setting fire to them (Thank goodness for the modern day hot water bottle!)

Farm Shop

We are lucky to have a well stocked farm shop near us that sells a lot more than just meat, because well- we are both vegetarians so we'd be out of luck. Its fun to see what new produce and posh snacks they have in- I love browsing the latest chutney flavours, and the posh crisps.

Local Woodland walk

What better time to get outside when the leaves are crunchy and the air is cool, but not freezing! Seeing all the beautiful autumn colours, the foliage getting ready to take its autumn nap until Spring. In my humble opinion a good woodland walk is best paired with a stop off at a traditional pub for something warm and hearty. After all, you've earned it after all that walking!

Visit a Brewery/Gin Distillery

If you live close to one of these, or you're happy to travel, this could be a fun day trip. A chance to learn all about how your favourite alcohol is made, and of course the obligatory taste testing that goes along with it! You might even find a new favourite.

At Home Ideas

Hot Chocolate Bar

Making a Hot Chocolate Bar is one of my favourite mini projects of the year. I use a surface in my kitchen that is otherwise a bit useless- its small, and has a cupboard above and below it, so not much height or depth to work with- but perfect for a hot chocolate bar. You might like to clear a small area on a work bench, or get an inexpensive bar cart if space is more limited.

Hot Chocolate Mix

- 1 Cup Icing Sugar
- 1 Cup Powdered Skimmed Milk
- ½ Cup Cocoa

Sieve it all together, then place in an airtight jar. I got some Kilner style clip top ones from Poundland a few years back and they are perfect!

Vegan/Lactose Intolerant friends- you can now get powdered oat milk that I reckon would work well in this recipe.

Extras

- Flavoured Syrups- I'm a Black Forest girl through and through.
- Sprinkles- Head to the Home Baking Section and grab those little jars!
- Candy Canes
- Spray Cream
- Mini Marshmallows
- Chocolate Chips

Halloween Movies

Halloween is absolutely my favourite day- its also my wedding anniversary! Halloween is a big deal in our house, but more on that later. I spend a large portion of October watching Halloween films- but not the scary kind (Unless I'm alone as Husband doesn't like them) I prefer spoopy Halloween films anyway- Some of my favourites are

- Halloweentown- All of them! (Even the one with Sara Paxton)
- Twitches (Tia and Tamera of Sister Sister fame as witches)
- Hocus Pocus- 1 and 2
- Kiki's Delivery Service

- The Craft (Were you even a 90s child if you didn't try and change your hair colour with magic after watching this?)
- Practical Magic

Make S'mores (Sans Campfire)

I was a bit obsessed with S'mores as a kid growing up watching American TV. They looked delicious, but we never went camping (Never will either, that's not for me) so I never really tried making them. Then one day a few years back I came across a recipe on the Aldi website of all places, with how to make S'mores in the microwave. So apologies to the S'mores purists out there, but for the camping averse, here's how.

<u>You will need</u>

- A pack of Chocolate Butter Biscuits
- Giant Marshmallows

1. Put a giant marshmallow between two butter biscuits.
2. Press down, then microwave in 10 second bursts until you have a gooey delicious S'more.

Warning- this is SERIOUSLY messy. Your hands will be super sticky so probably best to not be near your sofa or anything else that you don't want to accidentally touch and stain!

Friendsgiving

Confession- I've never actually done this, but I think it could be a really fun way to hang out with friends so I'm going to include it here. Its obviously a take on the traditional American Thanksgiving, but rather than the high stress stakes of cooking a big meal for your family and the drama that accompanies it (I'm reliably informed from an American friend this is how it often goes) it's a more relaxed affair with the family you have chosen. You could go traditional and do all the cooking, but I think it would be more fun and less stressful to have everyone bring something. That way you can actually spend time with your friends, rather than being stuck in the kitchen or in hostess mode. You can absolutely make this a celebration all your own- get the board games out, watch a film or just chat on the sofa with a glass of wine or hot chocolate. Its up to you!

Board Game Night

Board games are underrated fun in my opinion. I think a lot of people have bad memories of Monopoly and are hesitant to give them another go. Fun fact there is a HUGE world of games beyond Monopoly, Cluedo and the like. For the hardcore among you, there's Catan. Be prepared to sacrifice days of your life to play that! If you're new to board games there are definitely less time intensive and complicated options.

- Mysterium- A spooky cluedo-esque game
- Wingspan- Collect and look after birds.
- Terraforming Mars- For my fellow Sci Fi fans.
- Ticket to Ride- Build train routes before your friends sabotage them.
- Betrayal at House on the Hill- Build a haunted house whilst finding out which one of your friends is the traitor.

CHAPTER 3

Autumn Baking

Baking is a year round occurrence in my household. At least a few times a month you'll find me in the kitchen whipping up everything and anything from muffins, to biscuits to tiered cakes. I have very fond memories of baking with my nan, and baking now makes me feel connected to her, even though she has long since passed. I think there's something extra lovely about baking in the Autumn. For one, having to reach into a hot oven to pull out your baked goods in the middle of Summer is not exactly fun. Also, lets be honest- we are all craving some sugary carb based treats on those chilly, rainy autumn days! The smell of freshly baked goods wafting throughout your home is just heavenly (I am now reminded of that scene from Clueless where Cher narrates the tips she is following to have a perfect date with Christian, which includes "You should always have something baking in the oven" When she inevitably forgets to take it out and it burns, Chrisitans flawless response of "Aw Honey, you baked!" gets me EVERY time)

Nineties nostalgia aside, If baking for you involves grabbing a packet mix, that's absolutely fine! We are busy people, with busy lives and sometimes that's all we have the energy and time for. But if you'd like to have a go at baking from scratch, here are some of my favourite bakes.

Cinnamon Rolls

I adore Cinnamon rolls, but we seem a bit obsessed with the pastry kind here in the UK, not the proper bread kind! Here's my go to small batch recipe which makes 4 rolls (Perfect for 2 people, but the recipe is easily doubled!)

You will need

- 15cm Diameter Baking Dish

For the Dough

- 80ml Milk
- 1 teaspoon active dry yeast
- 1 tablespoon granulated sugar plus a pinch for proofing yeast
- 2 tablespoons salted butter melted and slightly cooled
- 1 large egg yolk
- ¼ teaspoon salt
- 150g bread flour

For the Filling

- 70g packed brown sugar
- 1 teaspoon cinnamon
- 2 tablespoons salted butter, softened

Pro tip- Get a food thermometer. It will dramatically increase your chances of getting your yeast to work!

Pour your milk into a mug and microwave it for about 30 seconds then pop your thermometer in. It should read between 40c-45c (105f-115f) If It doesn't, microwave in shirt bursts until it does.

Stir in the yeast and a pinch of sugar and allow to sit for 10-15 minutes until the top of the mixture looks foamy.

In a bowl, whisk together milk and yeast mixture with the melted butter, sugar, egg yolk, and salt. Pop your dough blade in your processor, or your dough hook for a stand mixer, and pour the liquid in to the bowl.

Add the flour and process until a thick, sticky dough forms and all the flour is incorporated. In a food processor this will happen very quickly- don't be tempted to keep pulsing as you run the risk of killing the yeast due to the speed of the blade making everything hot.

Drop the mixture onto a well-floured work surface and knead gently until the dough is no longer sticky and comes together into a ball.

Place dough into a greased bowl, cover with a cling film or a towel, and allow to rise in a warm place for an hour to 90 minutes, until doubled in size. If its a particularly chilly day your airing cupboard is a great place for your dough to rise! If using cling film, save it when you take it off after the dough has proved as you can re use it on your second rise.

Once your dough has risen, turn it out on a lightly floured surface and slowly stretch it rectangular shape, and then use a rolling pin to roll the dough out to about 12cm by 40cm. Gently manipulate the corners and sides so you have a nice rectangle.

Stir together brown sugar and cinnamon.

Spread the melted butter over the entire thing and top with the brown sugar mixture. Roll into a tight log from the short side. Keep it as tight as you can for that amazing shape when baked!

Use a serrated knife to cut the roll into 4 pieces. Don't use a butter knife here or the shape will be off.

Place the rolls in a 15cm greased baking dish. Cover with your saved cling film or towel, place them in a warm spot, and allow to rise for 45 minutes to an hour, until they look puffy.

Preheat oven to 190c/Gas Mark 5.

Bake cinnamon rolls for 15-22 minutes, until the tops look golden.

Allow rolls to cool for a few minuted before pouring on glace icing.

If you want to freeze these, hold off on the icing and let them cool fully. Wrap tightly in foil, and pop in a freezer bag to ensure they don't get freezer burn. Defrost thoroughly overnight before popping in the microwave for 30seconds to a minute.

Honey Oat Loaf

Home made bread is always a winner, but this Honey Oat loaf is particularly delicious this time of year and makes excellent toast.

You will need:

- 9"x5" Loaf Tin
- A bowl

For the Loaf

- 375g Bread Flour
- 60g Oats
- 1 Packet Instant Yeast
- 1 tsp Salt
- 250ml Milk
- 60ml Warm Water (Around 45c)
- 30g Unsalted Butter
- 85ml Honey, warmed

For glaze

- 40ml Honey, warmed
- 30g Porridge Oats (NOT instant!)

1. Combine Oats, Flour, Yeast and Salt in a bowl.
2. Heat Butter and Milk until melted. Allow to cool a little, then add the honey and water.
3. Add wet ingredients to dry, and knead by hand for about 10 minutes (Or use a dough hook attachment if you have a mixer)
4. Put your dough in an oiled bowl, and let rise until its doubled in size- about an hour.

5. Shape your loaf and put it into a 9" x 5" loaf tin, and let it rise another hour.
6. Preheat Oven to Gas 4 / 180c.
7. Spread Honey on top of loaf and sprinkle with oats.
8. Bake for 40-50mins until golden.
9. Allow to cool completely, then slice and enjoy!

Pumpkin Spice Cake

You know I love me some Pumpkin Spice- this sheet pan cake with cream cheese frosting is delicious, and freezes well if you can't get through 12 slices in a couple of days.

- 280g Plain Flour
- 2 teaspoon baking powder
- 2 teaspoon cinnamon
- ¾ teaspoon ground nutmeg
- ¾ teaspoon ground cloves
- ½ teaspoon ground ginger
- ½ teaspoon salt
- 4 large eggs, at room temperature
- 300 grams granulated sugar
- 225 grams unsalted butter
- 1 tin pumpkin purée

<u>Cream Cheese Frosting</u>

- 1 package of full-fat cream cheese (around 200g size), softened to room temperature
- 115g unsalted butter, softened to room temperature
- 360g Icing sugar,
- 1 teaspoon pure vanilla extract

Pro Tip- If you're all out of time/energy after baking the cake, a pack of supermarket cream cheese frosting works too.

1. Preheat Oven to Gas 4 / 180c
2. Grease a 9" x 13" Tin, and line the bottom with

baking paper.
3. Sift together the dry ingredients.
4. Whisk eggs and sugar for approximately 2 minutes with an electric whisk until the mixture looks thick and pale yellow.
5. Add melted butter and pumpkin to this mixture and whisk for about a minute.
6. Add in the dry ingredients and mix by hand with a spatula to avoid overworking the batter.
7. Put batter in tin and bake 30-35mins until a toothpick comes outs clean.
8. Allow to cool completely In the tin before removing and slicing.

Frosting

Mix the butter and cream cheese together with an electric whisk until fully combined.

Add in the vanilla, and the sugar a bit at a time (to avoid a cloud of icing sugar in your kitchen!)

CHAPTER 4

Autumn Meals

I have a confession to make... I eat comfort food year round. It could be a hot summers day, and I will still happily eat sausages and mash! I'm not salad averse *per se*, but I really don't feel any inclination to "eat lighter" in the summer- my body must have missed the memo on that one.

I feel like comfort food is such a British thing. This isn't to say that other countries don't have their own hearty food (Mac 'n' Cheese, Pot Roast my American friends?) but no one does it quite like the Brits! From hearty stews and casseroles, to pie and mash, we all love a bit of carb based goodness.

Lets not forget the vegetables though- Autumn means delicious root vegetables like Carrots, Parsnip, Swede and others such as Squash, Pumpkin, Cabbage and Cauliflower. Autumn fruits include Apples and Pears, and the much maligned Quince.

Everyone has their favourite comfort foods of course, here are some of mine.

Root Vegetable Curry

Serves 4

- 2 Tbsp Oil
- 1 Onion, Diced
- 2 Garlic Cloves, Crushed
- 700g Potatoes, peeled and sliced into chunks

- 4 Carrots, peeled and thickly sliced
- 2 Parsnip, peeled and thickly sliced
- 2 Tbsp Curry Paste (I use Pataks Balti)
- 1 Litre Veg Stock
- 100g Red Lentils

Step 1

Heat the oil in a large saucepan and cook the onion and garlic over a medium heat for 3-4 minutes until softened. Add in the potatoes, carrots and parsnips, turn up the heat to medium and cook for 6-7 minutes, stirring, until the vegetables look golden.

Step 2

Stir in the curry paste, add in the stock give it a stir then bring to the boil. Reduce the heat, add the lentils, cover and simmer for 15-20 minutes until the sauce has thickened and the vegetables have softened.

Serve with warm Naan.

PS- This freezes really well if you want to make a batch of it.

Spicy Sausage Chilli

Serves 2-3

- 2 tbsp Oil
- 1 onion, diced
- 2 garlic cloves, crushed
- Pack of Taco seasoning
- 500g Passata
- 400g tin black beans, drained and rinsed
- 1 tbsp light soft brown sugar
- 6 Cumberland-style bangers (meat or plant based)
- 100g Lightly Salted Tortilla Chips

Step One

Preheat Oven to Gas 6 / 200c.
Heat the oil in a flameproof casserole dish or ovenproof saucepan over a low-medium heat. Lightly fry the sausages. Once cooked cut them into thirds diagonally. Set aside.

Fry the onion and garlic for 5 mins until softened. Add the fajita seasoning, stir to coat and cook for a minute or so more.

Step Two

Add the Passata, black beans, brown sugar and sausages. Stir gently to combine.
Pop in the oven with a lid on for 15 minutes.

Step Three

Meanwhile, lightly crush the Tortilla chips with your hands. You don't want crumbs, just smaller bits! Remove the Chilli from the oven, scatter with Tortilla chips then pop back in oven for 5 minutes, without lid, to brown the topping a bit. Serve!

Do not Freeze.

Leftovers, minus Tortilla chips, keep well in the fridge for a day or two.
If you leave the tortilla chips in, they may go a bit soggy, but still fine to eat.

Baked Bean Cottage Pie

Serves 4

1 Tbsp Oil
500g Mince (I use plant based)
3 Garlic cloves, crushed
1 Onion, diced
1 Carrot, diced
Tin of Peas (Or equivalent weight of frozen peas)
Tin of Baked Beans
OXO Beef Cube (I use meat free version)

1 tsp Mixed Herbs
2 Tbsp Hendos (or Worcestershire sauce)
800g Mashed Potato (Store bought, or your own!)

Step One

Preheat Oven to Gas 6 / 200c.

Fry onion, garlic and carrot for 6-8 mins until softened.
Add in mince, cook for 12-15 minutes. If using meat mince, drain excess oil after cooking.
Add in beans, peas, crumbled OXO cube, herbs and Hendos and let it simmer for a few minutes over medium heat.

Step Two

Pop the mix into an oven proof dish, top with mash- running your fork over it to create wavy lines, and cook for approximately 30 minutes until topping is crisp.

Serve with veg. (I like green beans)

This freezes really well if you want to batch it!

Vegan Ma Po

Serves 2

400g "meat free" pieces (Supermarket own vegan brand are perfect!) or Firm Tofu, cubed
1 tbsp corn flour
125ml Water
1 tbsp Oil
2 Garlic Cloves, crushed
1 Tsp fresh ginger grated, or ginger paste
25g Onion, diced (Frozen diced onions mean no waste for a small amount!)
80g Sweetcorn
80g Frozen Peas
1 tsp Sichuan Peppercorn powder (If you have whole peppercorns,

grind them)
1 tbsp Soy Sauce
1.5 tbsp Gojuchang Paste (Any spicy chilli bean paste you can find will work)

Cooked rice, to serve. (Microwave rice for a mid week rush win!)

Step One

Cook the meat free pieces in oven according to instructions. If using Tofu, make sure its ready to be added straight to the pan later!

Mix the cornflour and water and keep to one side for now.

Step Two

Heat the oil in a wok or large frying pan. Fry the onion, garlic and ginger for a few minutes until softened. Add the corn and peas and fry for a few minutes more.

Step Three

Add in the chilli paste and Sichuan pepper. Stir it together with the veg, then add in the meat free pieces from the oven (Or Tofu if that's what you're using), along with the water cornflour mix and soy sauce.
Simmer it all for a few minutes, then serve with rice.

Can be Frozen (Not the rice)

Makes excellent leftovers- please be cautious if reheating cooked rice to ensure its hot enough to kill any bacteria that may be present.

Giant Sausage Roll

Serves 4

1 Sheet Puff Pastry
6 plant based sausages (ones without casing) OR 200g sausage meat

3 tbsp chutney (Red Onion is my favourite)

Step One

Preheat Oven Gas 4/180c.

If using plant based sausages- pop them in a bowl and mash them up with your hands! Squidge it together.

Step Two

Unroll the pastry sheet. Put the sausage meat in the middle of the sheet so its parallel to the long side of the pastry.
Use your hands to flatten and shape the meat into a long rectangle, making sure its not too flat. Top it with the chutney.

Step Three

Slice the pastry either side of the sausage meat diagonally, making several strips.
Fold the ends of the pastry up to the meat, then alternate putting your diagonal strips across the top. Once its all covered pop it in the oven for 40 minutes.

Serve with veg of your choice.

Freezes well. Reheat in the oven from frozen at Gas 6/200c for 25-30 mins.

CHAPTER 5

Autumn Cleaning

Spring cleaning is ok and all, but Autumn cleaning is where its AT. Think about it, you're preparing to spend months predominantly inside your home, isn't that a great reason to want to freshen it up? Its hard to feel cosy and relaxed when there's cobwebs about and its not Halloween!

So I'm going to assume that you know how to clean, so rather than include all the basic day to day jobs you already do I've just put down the bigger, less frequent or neglected jobs we are all guilty of not doing.

Checklist

Living Room

- Wash cosy blankets
- Wash Removable Cushion Covers
- Clean Upholstered/Leather furniture.
- Clean Rugs (Professionally if they are upmarket ones like a real Persian Rug)
- Clean Fireplace (Get your chimney sorted too if its a real one!)
- Pull out all the furniture to clean behind it
- Dust Baseboards

Kitchen

- Oven Clean (Call someone in if you hate it as much as I do)
- Check Extractor Filter
- Clean inside Fridge
- Clean Fridge Coils
- Defrost Freezer as necessary
- Check for out of date/nearing its best date cans/tins/packets. I will eat food past its best, but on a case by case basis!
- Dust Baseboards

Hallway

- Check Smoke Alarm / Carbon Monoxide Detector
- Swap Summer shoes for Autumn shoes

Bathroom(s)

- Clean inside cabinets
- Take expired medication to the Pharmacy for disposal
- Bin any out of date or past their best beauty products

Bedroom(s)

- Move furniture so you can clean behind it and underneath it
- Dust Baseboards
- Clean Curtains (Check the label, steam cleaners are great if too delicate to wash)

Additionals

Get your boiler serviced! Seriously you don't want it breaking down at this time of year.

Add Thermal liners to curtains for extra warmth, or swap to thicker curtains

Dig out your draught excluders, or pick some up- they are relatively inexpensive.

If you use a portable gas heater, make sure you've got plenty of gas in your bottle.

Log burner? Check you've got enough fuel and kindling. Solar? We're all jealous!

CHAPTER 6

Autumn Reflections

Autumn to me is **the** time of year to do a little self reflection. The dark evenings, cloudy days and a sense that everything around us is having a well earned rest before the busy-ness of Spring time. All these things invite us inward, to go deep below the surface and see what lies there.

Journaling is a great tool for reflection. There's something satisfying about getting all those thoughts out of your head, seeing them in front of you and having some control about what happens next. When thoughts, worries and problems swirl around our heads they have a tendency to become overwhelming. What starts as a minor setback or inconvenience becomes an insurmountable hill that we don't see any point in climbing. We've become too close to the problem, we need to step back and take a breath.

Sometimes I will just freewrite- everything, anything in my brain just gets put onto paper. No one else is going to see it, but putting that distance between 'them' (the whirling thoughts) and me (My logical self) really helps me to calm down. When I go back and read what I have written I am more clear headed, and can look at things in a more logical way. That insurmountable hill becomes much more approachable.

Sometimes I prefer to use a journaling prompt, particularly if I'm feeling a bit out of sorts, but I cant really put a finger on why. Or if I want to focus on something more specific rather than a general de-jumble of my thoughts.

If you've never tried journaling, go grab that shiny notebook (that you most definitely did not purchase in the back to school sale) a pen, and a cup of something hot. Get comfortable, and let all the whirly swirly thoughts out! If you're not really sure what to write, you could try some of these prompts to get started. Don't worry if you feel like you've gone off track- they're prompts, not essay questions!

Autumn Specific Prompts

- What is it about Autumn that you love the most? What makes it special for you?
- How did you feel about Autumn as a child? How is that the same/different as now?
- What things can you do during Autumn that will inspire you, and lift you up?
- What do you want to let go of this season? What do you want to keep?
- Is there something you dread at this time of year? If so, what can you do to minimise it?

General Prompts

- What is something that you can do right now to simplify your life?
- What's one step you can take towards a bigger problem you're facing?
- If you were living your dream life right now, what would that look like?
- What would you like to tell someone who is no longer here?
- What advice would you give your teenage self?

Self Discovery Prompts

- Whats something I know now, that I didn't know a year ago?

- What distracts me when I want to be productive?
- What makes me feel good about myself?
- How would my friends describe me?
- How does my body feel, right now?

Morning Pages

I touched on this briefly in the Morning Routine chapter, but I'm going to go into a bit more depth here. Morning Pages are a way of essentially "brain dumping" each morning and were made popular by Julia Cameron, author of The Artists Way. Morning pages for Cameron are an essential tool for the recovering Artist, a way to clear out the messy thoughts and concerns of our waking self so we can create our art free of distractions. However, the concept has garnered popularity with people from all walks of life, artists or not, and many people consider it an essential practice in their life that helps them start the day on the right foot.

Cameron stated that morning pages should be three, full size loose leaf pages and that you should write anything that pops into your head. Even if that's "I don't know what to write" over and over. She advocated that these pages should be stored away, preferably in a Manila envelope, and not be looked at again.

For me, the thought of filling three pages of lined paper with words at six in the morning is well.. a bit much. Its anxiety inducing if I'm being completely honest. I would actively avoid it every time I re-read the book.

Instead, I give myself permission to do it my way.

And you should too.

Maybe it just one page.
Maybe its a paragraph.
Maybe its a note on your phone.

The most important thing, is that it works for you. Maybe morning pages aren't right for you and that's fine. I'd recommend giving them a go to see how you feel, but if it doesn't work that's ok! I'm including it here as I feel its a great tool for reflection if you break Cameron's rule of not looking at them. I wouldn't advise looking at them right away. Give it some time and when you do look back, I bet you'll be surprised at what you find on those pages!

CHAPTER 7

Autumn Scents

Is there anything cosier than snuggling up with a blanket, a hot drink and a scented candle, wax melts or diffuser going? Scent is a powerful sense- how often have you found yourself remembering a happy time at the beach when the smell of fresh doughnuts is in the air? Everyone has their favourites, and quite often scents they detest. I'm very much a sweet scent person- vanilla, caramel, chocolate! Perhaps you're more floral, woody or citrusy? Either way I hope you'll find some inspiration further on when I share blends you can create yourself.

Autumn is a season rich with scents- from the delights of petrichor (the smell after it rains) to the smell of crunchy, (then soggy) leaves- autumn really is a time for indulging our sense of smell. We typically spend much more time indoors, which is more than likely why we all rush out at this time of year to buy our favourite scented products.

I am a huge fan of scented candles, specifically Bath and Body Works candles that are now available in Next. They are huge, 3 wick candles that never disappoint on the scent front and from my experience, are never subject to tunnelling like some other brands. Yes they are expensive, and some find them overpowering but for me, they are the candle of the season! Next is now offering a limited selection of Bath and Body Works products in store (and online) so if you want to test the scents before purchasing, you can! Do check they are in your local store though. I found them in Westfields, or rather I drove there on the day they launched… because I was too excited not to!

Bath and Body Works has a huge array of scents- just search on eBay and you'll see what I mean! Some of my favourite scents are:

Merry Cookie- A sweet bakery smell with vanilla and caramel.

Pumpkin Pecan Waffles- Autumn baked goods in a jar. Enough said.

Hot Cocoa- Exactly what it says on the tin.

Mahogany Teakwood- Smells like shower gel from a certain brand marked "For Men" If you like masculine scents, this is the one for you. I get the high intensity version for maximum 'man smell' as my husband jokes! This is a bit out of left field for me as a sweet scent addict, but honestly I fell in love with it!

As mentioned they are pricey (Around £20-25) but they last for AGES. I only have a couple and I don't need to buy more anytime soon. Obviously if you burn them all day every day they wont last as long, but if you burn for a few hours at a time you'll get your moneys' worth. The smell lingers, so there's really no need to burn them continuously.

Yankee Candles are another favourite. If you have an outlet store nearby then its worth a visit to get a good deal. We bought the Argan Oil scent a few years back from our local outlet for a great price, and its still going!

If you're Vegan, or just environmentally conscious, I highly recommend Cosy Glow candles. They are made from Soy Wax and come in some great scents. Pumpkin Spice and Winter Spice are two of my favourites.

If candles aren't your thing (I know some people aren't keen on artificial scents) then an electric diffuser is a great alternative. I purchased one a few years back for around £20 and its great. You simply add water and essential oils, press the button and that's it- your room will be filled with an amazing, natural scent.

I have a huge collection of essential oils, and I love experimenting with blends for my diffuser. These are some of my favourites.

Autumn Sunday

8 Drops Thyme
4 Drops Patchouli
2 Drops Vanilla
1 Drop Jasmine

Autumn Spice

3 Drops Cardamom
3 Drops Cassia
3 Drops Cinnamon
1 Drop Vanilla

Autumn Leaves

3 Drops Tangerine
3 Drops Atlas Cedarwood
2 Drops Clove

Autumn Cheer

4 Drops Orange
3 Drops Nutmeg
2 Drops Lavender
2 Drops Ylang Ylang

Autumn Breeze

4 Drops Bergamot
3 Drops Cedarwood
2 Drops Clove

If you're feeling full of a cold, try this blend to help you feel less congested

Breathe Easy

3 Drops Eucalyptus
2 Drops Tea Tree
2 Drops Peppermint
1 Drop Lemon

Looking for more of a sweet scent? Try these for a home that smells like you baked!

Cinnamon Buns

5 Drops Orange
4 Drops Vanilla
3 Drops Cinnamon
1 Drop Cardamom

Christmas Cookies

3 Drops Vanilla
2 Drops Cinnamon
2 Drops Nutmeg
1 Drop Lemon

Freshly Baked Biscuits

6 Drops Cassia
5 Drops Orange
3 Drops Clove
3 Drops Nutmeg

If you prefer more of a clean smell to your home, these are for you!

Crisp and Clean

3 Drops Lime
3 Drops Eucalyptus
3 Drops White Fir

Clean and Sparkling

3 Drops Lemon
2 Drops Lemongrass

2 Drops Peppermint

Cleaning Motivation

4 Drops Peppermint
3 Drops Lavender
3 Drops Eucalyptus

Another way I like to use essential oils is in roll on blends. You can get roller bottles from Amazon, which are easy to fill with your own blend. Important note- you MUST use a carrier oil in these. Never, ever fill them with just essential oil and roll it on your skin! Essential oils undiluted are incredibly strong and can cause serious irritation. Carrier oils include oils such as Jojoba, Rose Hip, Sweet Almond and Argan oil.

Roll on blends are a great alternative to perfume for those who aren't keen on the strength of the scent, or the price tag! You can make your own blends but please do check as some essential oils should never be put directly on skin- even with a carrier oil. I've included a couple of my favourite blends below to take the guesswork out for you.

Based on a 10ml Rollerbottle.

Place oils in bottle, then top up with your carrier oil. **Please test a small amount of the blend on a non sensitive and easy to rinse area (e.g back of your hand) before applying**. Better to be safe than sorry, as some people will be more sensitive than others.

Motivate Me

4 Drops Orange
2 Drops Lime
2 Drops Black Peppermint
2 Drops Frankincense.

Head Tension Relief (Apply to temples and forehead)

2 Drops Peppermint

2 Drops Rosemary
2 Drops Eucalyptus
2 Drops Lavender

Calm Down

8 Drops Frankincense
10 Drops Lavender
6 Drops Cedarwood

Lift Me Up

13 Drops Grapefruit
8 Drops Orange
7 Drops Lemon

Sleepy Time

5 Drops Lavender
5 Drops Cedarwood

I really hope you get a chance to try some of these blends for yourself, I hope you enjoy them as much as I do. If nothing else, I hope you now go and light your favourite candle or wax melt to fill your home with your favourite scent!

CHAPTER 8

Autumn Films and TV

If ever there was a more perfect time to snuggle on the sofa and watch a film or TV series, its Autumn (Ok, Winter too) Especially on those slightly drab and cloudy days where you don't really fancy a walk in the woods, or being outside at all.

Autumn used to be *the* time, way back when terrestrial tv was a thing, that new TV shows would start. By this point you had been waiting months to start a new season, to see how the writers resolved *that* cliffhanger that you had been texting your friends about since it happened. Nowadays with the advent of streaming services, on demand television there's *always* something new to watch (Ironically, the chances of a cliffhanger getting resolved have dropped drastically due to streaming services relentlessly cancelling shows halfway though a season) so the anticipation has all but disappeared.

That isn't to say you can't recreate the vibe that comes from watching TV shows and Films this time of year. We all have our favourites of course, but here are some of mine.

- Gilmore Girls (You knew this would be top of the list)
- The Good Witch
- Charmed (I prefer the original, but the reboot is an option too)
- AHS: Coven
- Sweet Magnolias

There's plenty more of course depending on whether you like things more scary, or more small town wholesome.

Films are the mainstay of Autumn for me- I like having more time to get into a story, and the world that's been created to tell it. Also, there's no waiting around for an ending like you get with series that are ongoing. Two hours or so, and its all wrapped up.

I mentioned a few films earlier, but those were more Halloween specific. If you're after something that's more of a general cosy vibe, I recommend:

- Practical Magic
- When Harry Met Sally
- You've Got Mail
- Mystic Pizza
- Mona Lisa Smile
- Kiki's Delivery Service

Yes- these are all pre 2000's films. I haven't really watched anything recently that captures the cosy feels as much as these older films. Maybe I'm just old?

Cosy Film/TV Essentials

- Soft Blanket
- Cosy PJ's and Socks
- Hot Chocolate (Add Cinnamon for cosy vibes, or chilli for a spicy kick)
- Popcorn (Sweet for me, thanks)
- Posh Crisps (For Savoury snack lovers)

CHAPTER 9

Autumn Favourites

I'm sure that all of us Autumn lovers have a list of favourites. Things that when we see them we just think of cosy days, crisp leaves and all things Autumn. I've mentioned a fair few throughout this guide, but here is a comprehensive, all in one place list- because everyone loves a list!

Pumpkin Spice Latte

Shocking I know! My husband and I have an annual tradition of going to Starbucks and getting a PSL on the first weekend they are out. Or rather, I get a PSL and he gets tea because he hates coffee. Its a fun tradition, one I always post on Facebook so I can look back on the memories section each year. However, as much as I LOVE them, I actually limit myself to no more than three in the season they are out. I can hear you now- "Why? Why would you do that? They're the BEST!" A few reasons actually. First off- Starbucks is not cheap. I actually don't buy take away coffee at any other time of the year. I have a Nespresso at home, so I don't feel the need to spend £5 on a coffee- I'm pretty frugal at heart. Second- Its 10 miles to the nearest Starbucks so its massively out of my way to go get a coffee. Lastly, and most importantly, I don't want to have PSL for the sake of it. I want to really enjoy each one I have, to savour every bit of syrupy goodness.

Faux Fur Blanket

A couple of years ago I received what is possibly the worlds softest blanket in my Fab Fit Fun subscription box. Its silver, big enough to cover my legs to my waist and it's the cosiest blanket I've ever owned. It lives in my living room in a wicker basket that has a rabbit face (An Aldi Baby Event special buy, kids get all the best stuff) and is in use pretty much every day in Autumn and Winter.

Scented Candles

Bath and Body works is my go to as previously mentioned. Whilst they have a good range in Next, I do more often than not find myself on eBay buying them (or at least looking) as they have a much wider variety of scents. Yes, they are super expensive as the seller needs to cover their costs in getting them here, and turn a profit, but I can't help it, I love them!

My favourite Vegan brand is London based Cosy Glow. They make gorgeous Soy candles in a variety of scents. I have Winter Spice, Pumpkin Spice and Pine Needle They come in cute glass jars, and don't seem to tunnel like other brands I've had. Bonus- they're a small business and I try where at all possible to support small businesses over large faceless corporations.

Cosy Loungewear

Fun fact- I live in loungewear year round. Unless I'm in the outside world (As me and my fellow introvert Husband jokingly refer to it) I'm in loungewear. I know the school of thought about getting dressed for the day, and how it makes you feel more productive and put together. Honestly? What I wear has zero impact on my ability to be productive. I'm wearing Pyjamas right now, writing this book. I wore them this morning cleaning the bathroom and steam mopping my floors. I'll be wearing them when I cook dinner from scratch later! If wearing "proper" clothes at home works for you, go for it. But cosy loungewear, even if just reserved for weekends indoors for you, is a must for me. I bought a dusky pink jumpsuit from the Mrs Hinch range of loungewear in Tesco a few yeas back, and its my absolute favourite. I put a soft cotton lace trim cami top underneath (It gapes a little with the crossover style) and fuzzy socks on my feet and I am good to go (Potter around the house that is)

Baking

Baking is my jam (Pun intended) I bake year round, but in Autumn I kick it up a notch. Is there anything better than your house smelling like fresh baked bread? Don't get me wrong, I'm not one for making my own bread every week but I do like whipping up a loaf of Honey Oat Bread, Cinnamon Rolls or Pumpkin Sheet Cake (See Chapter 3 for recipes). I recently brought a used breadmaker for £10, and it might be the best £10 I ever spent. Seriously, the amount of time and effort saved!

I always bake at least one thing with pumpkin. Tinned pumpkin is still not really a thing here in the UK, but you can sometimes find it in bigger supermarkets in the USA food section. Failing that, Amazon has it. Buy it in advance though, as the price goes up in Autumn. You can of course get a fresh pumpkin and contend with all the guts, but that's not something I want to do!

Fuzzy Socks

I'm currently wearing a pair of socks that my mum bought for me about six years ago. She has since passed, and these socks are one of the last gifts I still have from her. So for me, these socks are more than just socks, they are a connection, a memory. Now your socks may just be fuzzy socks, and that's fine. I can't bear having cold feet, fuzzy socks keep my feet toasty and for extra cosy points I tuck my the bottom of my pyjama pants in to them! I also have a fabulous pair of stripy knee high socks that were a gift from my husband, who tracked down an American company who make socks for us tall folk who otherwise find knee high socks stopping mid calf.

Tea and Biscuits

I spent my late teen years living with my grandparents and every day at 3pm we would have a cup of tea and biscuits.

Every.Single.Day. And it was glorious! I have kept up this tradition over the years, and I enjoy it immensely. Is it the healthiest choice? No. Do I care? Also no! Though this is something I do most of the year, it feels cosier in Autumn and I might even splurge on a chocolate biscuit!

Roast Dinner

In our house we have Roast Dinner every Sunday lunchtime from late September through the last Sunday of November. I don't make it in December so as to build anticipation for Christmas lunch. We're vegetarians, so I cant speak to roasting a chicken or beef joint, but roast dinner for us comes together in a little over an hour so it doesn't feel like I spend my whole Sunday in the kitchen- and that one hour or so of effort is absolutely worth the end result. I avoid roast dinners in restaurants at all costs. They never ever taste good to me!

Boots

I own one pair of boots. That's it. To be fair, its all I need. They are black faux suede and a looser style. I love wearing them with skinny jeans and my houndstooth coat. So chic.

Hot Chocolate

Hot Chocolate is serious business in our house. Every October I set up a Hot Chocolate bar in our kitchen- I even make my own hot chocolate blends! In all honesty its cheaper per serving, and its just cocoa, icing sugar (It dissolves quicker and tastes sweeter than granulated) and milk powder. I also set out mini marshmallows, Monin syrups, various sprinkle jars from the baking section of the supermarket and in the fridge you will find both plain and chocolate squirty cream.

CHAPTER 10

HALLOWEEN

Halloween is my absolute *favourite* celebration of the year. Don't get me wrong, Christmas is great but seeing as I have no religious tie to it, its just a day of gift giving and great food that we do because well... everyone else does. That's fine, and I know most people are way more into Christmas, but not me.

Halloween is also my Wedding Anniversary, so its extra special to me. It was fate really, the year we got married Halloween was on a Saturday! I didn't have a spooky theme, but I loved it all the same.

<u>The Origins of Halloween</u>

Halloween is the modern day celebration adapted from Samhain (Pronounced sow-en) which was celebrated by the Celts about 2000 years ago. They believed that on this day the veil between the worlds of the living and the dead were at their thinnest, and that the spirits of the deceased could return. In the agricultural calendar it also marked the end of Summer and Harvest, and the move into Winter.

They lit huge bonfires to ward off the spirits, and the hearth of each home would be lit from it. This partly explains our modern custom for putting tea lights in pumpkins- though the use of Pumpkins is an import from our American friends. A Turnip would be considered a more traditional vegetable for this here in the UK.

With the advent of the Roman Empire and Christianity, the day eventually became All Souls Day in an attempt to blend Celtic and Christian beliefs, with the day before being known as All Hallows Eve, The tradition of bobbing for Apples is believed to be a nod to the Roman Goddess of fruit and tress Pamona.

Decorating

I am not a fan of the typical orange/black/purple/green colours, which makes finding decor a bit tricky! I adore Pastel Halloween, it's my whole girly girl vibe. Pastel Pumpkins, Spoopy Bats, Glittery signs.. *that's* my Halloween. I don't go OTT with it though, a few carefully placed pieces, plus the obligatory pastel Happy Halloween banner and I'm a happy girl. Places I've had success finding pastel Halloween decor are Etsy (Duh!) T.K Maxx, Next, Poundland and B&M's.

Halloween Recipes

Pumpkin Pancakes

- 450g peeled pumpkin (or butternut squash), cut into 1cm cubes
- 1 tbsp oil
- 150g self-raising flour
- 150ml milk
- 2 medium eggs
- 10g salted butter

Method

1. Preheat oven to Gas 6 / 200c
2. Put cubes of Pumpkin or Butternut squash in a roasting tray with the oil, and roast for 20 minutes.
3. Meanwhile, combine the flour with a pinch of salt in a bowl and make a well in the centre.
4. Take the pumpkin/squash out of the oven and mash with a fork. Put it in a jug with the milk and eggs and

whisk to combine.
5. Add into the bowl and mix to a smooth batter.
6. Melt a small amount of the butter in a large frying pan over medium heat. Spoon the batter into the pan- you could make 4-5 smaller pancakes, or 2-3 bigger ones depending on the size of the pan, or just how you feel!
7. Cook for about 90 secs until you see bubbles on top, then carefully slip over and cook one more minute.

Tip- Keep warm in the oven, or cover with foil!

Bat Nachos

- Pack of Flour Tortillas
- Bat shaped cutter

For the Topping

- Salsa
- Cheese
- Jalapenos
- Whatever else you like to put on Nachos!

1. Use the cutter to cut the bats from the tortillas
2. Spray a baking sheet with oil, then arrange in a single layer.
3. Bake in the oven at Gas 4 / 180c for 8-10minutes, until crisp.
4. Arrange on a plate with your nacho toppings!

Mini Ghost Pizzas

- Ready Made Pizza Dough (Or you can make your own!)
- Pizza Sauce
- Mozzarella cheese
- Ghost Shaped Cutter

1. Roll out the dough, and use cutter to make ghost shapes.
2. Top each ghost with sauce and cheese. You could use olives cut up into small pieces for eyes, if you like olives!
3. Bake in the oven according to cooking instructions on the dough package.

Pumpkin Hummus with Crudites

- 500g Pumpkin
- Olive Oil
- 2 Garlic Cloves
- ½ Lemon, juiced
- 2Tbsp Tahini
- Tin of Chickpeas, drained
- Red Pepper, sliced
- Yellow Pepper, sliced
- Breadsticks/Pitta Chips

1. Cut the top off the pumpkin, about two-thirds of the way up. Remove the pumpkin seeds, then scoop the flesh out of the bottom and the lid.
2. Heat oven to Gas 6 / 200c. Cut the pumpkin flesh into pieces and put in a roasting tin with the garlic and a good amount of oil. Season, then bake for 45 mins until very tender. Leave to cool.
3. Tip the pumpkin into a food processor with any juices from the roasting tin and the garlic. Add the lemon juice, tahini paste and chickpeas. Season with salt and blend to a paste – add a little more oil if it's too thick.

Serve with the peppers, breadsticks and pitta chips.

No Fuss Pumpkin Pie

- Ready Made Sweet Pastry Case
- 3 large eggs
- 100 grams granulated sugar
- 65 grams light brown sugar
- 1 tin pure pumpkin puree
- 175 ml double cream
- 1 teaspoon vanilla extract
- 1 1/2 teaspoons ground cinnamon
- 1/2 teaspoon ground ginger
- 1/4 teaspoon ground cloves
- ½ teaspooon salt

Method

1. Preheat Oven to Gas 7 / 220c
2. Whisk eggs and both sugars together until smooth.
3. Add pumpkin puree, cream, vanilla, cinnamon, ginger, cloves, and the salt. Stir until combined.
4. Pour filling into prepared pasty crust. If you have leftover filling you can freeze it (or make more pie!)
5. Bake for 15minutes.
6. Reduce temperature to Gas 5 / 190c and bake for a further 35-45mins until a toothpick inserted comes out clean.
7. Allow to cool for at least two hours, before cutting into eight pieces and serving with your choice of accompaniment such as whipped cream!

Note- You can absoutely make your own pastry crust if you so wish! This is simply a time saving recipe, and meant for those of us who aren't great at making pastry!

Spooky Drinks

Spooky Punch

- 150ml orange juice
- Green liquid food colouring
- 2 tbsp grenadine

Combine all ingrdients in a glass and decorate with spooky sweets- think jelly snakes, jelly laces, etc.

Scary Smoothie

- 225g frozen summer fruits, defrosted
- 1 banana, peeled
- 300ml cranberry and raspberry juice

Put ingredients in a blender, blend until smooth then enjoy!

Pumpkin Spice Mocktail

- 1 Can Ginger Beer (Ginger Ale)
- 4 Tbsp Pumpkin Puree
- 1/2tsp Pumpkin Pie Spice
- 1/2tsp Vanilla Extract

Method

1. Divide Ginger Beer between two glasses.
2. Mix the pumpkin puree, spice and vanilla extract until well combined.
3. Add the puree mix to each glass.
4. Add ice!

On a more serious note

Halloween, (or Samhain as it was traditionally known) is traditionally a time for honouring ancestors and those that have passed. If you're looking for a bit more than spooky bats and movies this could be a great opportunity to bring a bit more meaning to this day. A common practice is to have a dumb supper- where you lay the table to eat but also leave a place for someone who has passed. A smaller version of this is to leave an offering of something that the person loved (A favourite food, even tobacco if they were a smoker) in a special place, or outside. You might like to spend a few minutes thinking about some of your favourite memories, or speak a prayer if that's something you are comfortable with doing.

However you celebrate Halloween (Or Samhain) I hope you have a fantastic day- you deserve it.

BONUS CHAPTER

7 DAY COSY CHALLENGE

Who doesn't love a challenge? There's a challenge for everything- Save X amount of money, do a certain workout, don't spend money... but how about a cosy challenge?

For 7 days why not try adding in one thing per day that makes you feel cosy, or gets your home ready for Autumn? I'm not going to give you a prescriptive list to follow because everyone is different, and not every idea in this book will work for everyone.

Here's some ideas for you:

Pick up a new Autumn scent candle, OR dig out one you already own and put it somewhere you will see it, and light it!

Make up some Hot Chocolate mix so you have it on hand for when the need for Hot Chocolate strikes. Alternatively pick up your favourite one from the supermarket.

Find your favourite blankets, give them a wash and set them out on your sofa ready to pull over your legs whilst reading a book or watching a film.

Speaking of cleaning- pick an area in your home to give a good deep autumn clean. (Not super fun I know, but we all do better in a clean space!)

Curate your own list of books/films/tv shows to watch over the Autumn period so you don't forget!

Cook a recipe from the Autumn Cooking section, or find one

online or in a cookbook that you like and make it! Bonus points if you double the recipe and freeze it for those can't be bothered days.

Bake something- no further explanation needed!

Dig out your halloween decorations and/or have a trip out to purchase something new to add to your collection. This is also a good time to see if anything is broken or worn out. Don't forget batteries for anything that lights up or moves.

Make up a batch of Pumpkin Pie Spice ready for baking and making your own PSL. Keep it in a sealed container and it will last ages.

Dig out your Autumn/Winter clothes ready for sweater weather. This is a good opportunity to check if anything is moth eaten, or in need of repair.

Book a day trip somewhere that feels cosy to you- or use one of my aforementioned suggestions.

Organise a get together with friends *a la* friendsgiving. Have everyone bring something (But co-ordinate it so you don't end up with 6 cakes and nothing else- or don't!)

Treat yourself to some new teas- you can even get PSL tea now! Chair is also a good blend for Autumn.

Make an Autumn bucket list of everything you want to do before Halloween comes.

****

This is where our time together ends. Thank you so much for choosing to buy this book, it means the world to me. Remember, if you want more cosy follow me on Instagram @melaniesteeleauthor

Wishing you the cosiest Autumn,
Melanie

ABOUT THE AUTHOR

Melanie Steele (she/her) is a late thirty something living in a cosy village in Buckinghamshire with her Husband. You'll most often find her in the Kitchen baking a recipe she found online on her phone, then cursing herself for not turning auto timeout off and thus getting her phone covered in flour when the screen goes black.

You can find her on Instagram @melaniesteeleauthor

Printed in Great Britain
by Amazon